RETHINKING AFRICAN CULTURES

CULTURES

A Case of the Nso People

By

DIVINE VERKIJIKA

DEDICATION

To humanity

CONTENTS

ACKNOWLEDGMENTS

To all my friends and colleagues whom I had to run this idea by
several times

INTRODUCTION

Culture is the totality of the way of life evolved by a people in their attempts to meet the challenge of living in their environment, which gives order and meaning to their social, political, economic, aesthetic and religious norms thus distinguishing a people from their neighbors

Bello (1991: 189)

The culture of Africa is varied and manifold, consisting of a mixture of countries with various tribes that each have their own unique characteristic from the continent of Africa. It is a product of the diverse populations that today inhabit the continent of Africa and the African Diaspora.

African culture is expressed in its arts and crafts, folklore and religion, clothing, cuisine, music and languages. Expressions of culture are abundant within Africa, with large amounts of cultural diversity being found not only across different countries but also within single countries.

Even though African cultures are widely diverse, they are also, when closely studied, seen to have many similarities. For example, the morals they uphold, their love and respect for their culture as well as the strong respect they hold for the gods they believe in and the important Kings and Chiefs.

Wikipedia

1. MY ROOF OR MY CULTURE

My grandfather, was a clan head (Biki), in the Nso Fondom in Cameroon. A modest man with several families under his supervision, who kept his obligations to his tradition and to the state.

One time he organized a "Death Celebration" (A traditional African culture to celebrate the deceased and ancestors in each family often done at least one or more years after their departure)

As custom demands, he invited the Ngiri, (a palace based all-male masquerade centered cult that amongst other things is entitled to being present at burials or death celebrations of its members)

Generally, where there is means, this cult of men and its masquerades comes to the venue at the eve of the event. They camp outside and spend the whole night playing traditional music and doing whatever rituals need to be done. In the night, only initiates are allowed to witness the events, but when its dawn, and family members and sympathizers have come, the cult begins to release its masquerades for public display.

They have several masquerades each built around a concept most often understood to initiates however these masquerades are always a source of entertainment or at least intrigue to the masses who often turn up to witness. Unlike cultural dances, these masquerades are often filled with glamour, mystery and even fright. Mostly just one masked individual, with agents to guide its movement, as the masquerades have to move around the compound and sometimes the whole neighborhood, to display.

One of such masquerades, which happens to be the most popular in the Ngiri sect, is the Wan Mabu, well known for its acrobatic displays, and a real crowd puller.

The uninitiated population is allowed to watch and follow around but not allowed to touch, for fear of several "spiritual" consequences which often leads to a very intriguing display whereby the masquerade runs towards the population, and the population has to run away before regathering, keeping themselves a distance away from the masquerade.

This death celebration was a huge event for the family, as it was dedicated to all deceased family members in more than a decade, for whom this ritual had not been done and the event would also bring allot of population to the big compound.

Because of the magnitude of the event, my grandfather with the help of his family put allot of energy into its organization, and sacrificed allot to be able to entertain the masquerades and the population, but amongst all, he sacrificed to put new aluminum sheets on his roof.

On that fateful day, this masquerade was released, and it displayed around the compound, everything was moving on well, then as it sometimes happens, the acrobatic masquerade, ran to the back of the house, climbed on a kola nut tree, with a cheering population anxiously watching, after some display on the tree, which was close to the wall of the house, the Wan Mabu, skipped from the tree and landed on my grandfather's new aluminum sheet roof.

My grandfather who was inside his chambers attending to special guests, heard the loud cheers and rushed out to see what was going on in his courtyard.

Once outside, he saw the masquerade on his rooftop, then he retreated into his chambers and returned outside immediately with a loaded den gun. He pointed the gun at the masquerade and angrily shouted "Get down from there, or I will shoot you. Do you know the cost of one bundle of aluminum roofing sheets?".

He was stern and determined to shoot. The magnificent, all feared and masquerade shamelessly went down from the roof, hovered around and then retired to its camp.

This incident caused allot of resentment on the part of the leaders of the masquerade who consequently reported my grandfather to the palace, which led to his suspension from palace activities.

This experience was a big shock and a topic of debate amongst the population; those who held their culture sacred saw it being desecrated and emasculated in public, while others, saw an old man who suffered to afford aluminum roofing sheets for his house, and was protecting his property from destruction and demanded reasonable behavior from the Juju community.

But to me, a bigger debate was in play; that of the role and relevance of a conservative African tradition in a competitive and evolving world.

Of course this was a decade ago, somethings have evolved, but my purpose is to evaluate to what extent and of what benefit if any?

DIVINE VERKIJIKA

2. OUR ASSETS & COMPROMISED VALUES

Culture has been classified into its material and non-material aspects. While material culture refers to the visible tactile objects which man is able to manufacture for the purposes of human survival; non-material culture comprises of the norms and values of the people.

The breadth and diversity of Africa is definitely an asset for its people. Being a conservative people, has helped us to protect our environment probably more than any other continent in the face of threats like global warming.

Our cooperative system allows people to help each other in building houses and work on farms as opposed to the Western individualistic model which sometimes undermines care for each other and increases economic inequality.

Values occupy a central place in a people's culture and no group of people can survive without a set of values which holds them together and guarantees their continued existence, However Most contemporary Africans find it difficult to adjust between their traditional beliefs in certain aspects of their culture and the supposedly modern mode of accepted behavior.

For example, If the palace is the sanctum and epitome, of our culture, then it should be able to represent the highest of our values and aspirations in every way. But when you look at areas like hygiene, infrastructure, accountability, efficiency, you find us lacking behind in relation to other cultures.

Our traditional beliefs and systems don't only end where they are practiced, but go deep to affect how we think, and how we behave which has a direct consequence on the results we produce and the place we stand in respect to other cultures.

A lack of scientific approach towards our culture, has given room, for superstition, unaccountability, unreliability, theft and charlatanism, compromising our core values as a people and kept our evolution stagnated.

Policy makers and actors, should look at ways to bridge the gap between traditional ideologies/practices and contemporal realities, to ease ease conversion of philosophy to practical action, Increasing accountability, effectiveness and efficiency, Creating records for present and future reference, Innovating and exporting some aspects of culture.

It's imperative that any local culture that wishes to survive should create local scientific commissions to find ways to employ the productive aspects of other cultures that we have and acquire those we need. Probably because most of the custodians of the tradition and culture often have limited formal education, and the tradition is often a source of income and social status for them, they tend to become biased towards the idea of bringing a written/scientific culture to the system.

3. TIMES ARE CHANGING, SO MUST WE

We need to understand that, the conditions in which the original tradition was created are no longer the same. For example, our country constitution, laws and international treaties now have more enforceable power than our customs and traditions.

In the past, each tribe under a king and a common language was a nation, and its tradition embodied both political, economic, spiritual and social aspects of their life. Today, the socio-economic, political, and even spiritual centers of our communities have moved away from the palace into, government, business, organized religion and developmental organizations.

Despite government recognition of our chiefdoms, as custodians of our culture and even sometimes representative of our people, judging by same government books, one can safely say that our chiefdoms have become more symbolic than powerful and that the survival of chiefdoms today has become an issue of private enterprise.

The only constant thing is life is change, and whatever refuses to evolve, degenerates and may even go extinct. However when one looks at how radically conservative some African tribes and even government policies towards arts and culture tend to be, one is tempted to ask if their idea is to lead our culture to extinction.

Conserving African Tradition in this era, is like sitting by the river and dying of thirst.

According the 2017 *Drivers of Migration and Urbanization in Africa* report by the United Nations, The continent is urbanizing more rapidly than any other part of the planet. Africa's 1.1 billion citizens will likely double in number by 2050, and more than 80% of that increase will occur in cities.

We know that where Cities succeed traditional Culture often degenerates in favor of urban culture as people come from varying backgrounds, and governments authority overrides local traditions, hence the African Cultures that will survive are those that will succeed to be urbanized or at least be sustainably managed.

Here are 2 glaring examples on how urbanization and tradition have been in conflict in among the Nso people.

Kumbo Water Crises: From 2015 - 2018 the main tap water supply company in Kumbo, had a serious case of dispute between the Nso Palace and the Kumbo Council, which almost divided the community into factions that haven't been easy to reconcile.

The Palace believes to be the rightful owner, of the water scheme and the council asserts that water supply is a question of community security and must be supervised by the council and puts in question the ability of the palace to effectively run such a delicate project.

The Jeng Palace: Some years ago in Nso land, a man decided to turn his home into a "palace", He created his own masquerades. The Nso people were against the idea of a new palace and decided to attack and burn down the place. The man took, the Nso Palace to court, and the palace was asked to pay for damages.

Irrespective of the outcomes of these conflicts, it is clear that times are changing, and that our tradition needs rethinking

What African Tradition is suffering from is no different from what religious organizations suffered from in Europe, when revolutionaries sought and won the war, to separate religion from the state. The only difference here is that religion found a way to thrive, while African tradition, in quest for conservatism is leading to possible extinction.

There is a wealth of sociocultural and economic value, within Traditional African Societies, that can not only be a source of wellbeing for Africans, but also a contribution to world heritage and human evolution.

However, for this to happen, the custodians of tradition, need to rethink their position, become more organized employ appropriate models, that permit them to exist and thrive in a competitive world.

The Custodians of the tradition must understand that people are no longer obliged to follow tradition just because it is tradition and must be ready, to develop strategies to win the population to its way of thinking. They must be able to rethink, redefine and fine-tune their offer to the public in ways that are appropriate for this generation.

African pastors in recent times are becoming some of the richest class of people in society. Churches, are investing today in better management, better sound systems, more enticing venues, well skilled musicians and skillfully integrating business and technological applications to enhance the experience of their members.

No Body is coming to safe African Tradition, not government, not organized religion, not even UNESCO. The best they will do is declare a world heritage site.

The palace, as custodian of tradition and culture will do better in this century, if it remains apolitical, and unaffiliated to organized religions and should be open to allowing people from other tribes and families to register and belong or benefit from its fellowships.

Palaces need register patents for their Masquerades, and other items of cultural and economic value and where possible give out exploitation licenses to companies and individuals that can afford to make a business out of it.

Palaces can be able to systematize and franchise some aspects and functions of their customs that are ready for public consumption.

The palace, could go into the business of producing, selling branded items of spiritual or cultural value including the fashion industry which has become a very lucrative business in the 21st century.

Palaces should be able to produce, manuals of best practices and of general information, such as traditional rituals, initiations into cults, procedures for traditional weddings, homecoming rituals and etc.

4. AFRICAN CULTURE & SPIRITUALITY

It's very difficult to separate African Culture from its spirituality, a mixture which often scares away a good number of people who prefer to adhere to other spiritual beliefs.

Stories and customs that should unite and inspire people, become redundant in Africa because we unnecessary mystify them. A mystery which often gives breathing space to fakery. Genuine custodians of African culture, should be able to stand against the charlatanism, that is general allowed to thrive around it.

African Traditions and Customs need a new pop culture, and its custodians need not be afraid, to lose control of some of it; People will always find new ways of doing things.

The culture of a people can be fragmented into social, moral, religious, political, aesthetic and economic values. We should be able to create commissions that can identify the distinct values of our culture, and promote or adapt each accordingly.

Culture grows either through Invention, discovery or diffusion. However the rate of invention within a society is a function of the size of the existing culture base, which means for us to increase the size of our culture base, we need to be open to welcoming aspects of other cultures.

Every human being is likely to become infused with the culture of the society he grows up in, whether knowingly or unknowingly and a people's development is hugely determined by their culture, even a people's technology is part of their culture. Hence for us to be able to move from one level of development to another we need to create a culture enables and promotes such development and this is very much dependent on our will and ability to yield to change.

DIVINE VERKIJIKA

5. CONCLUSSION

In his book, ***Intelligence and How to Get It: Why Schools and Cultures Count***, Richard Nisbett, a professor of social psychology at the University of Michigan, challenges the argument that IQ is entirely or almost entirely heritable, and argues that nonhereditary factors play a more significant role than hereditarianism asserts. He also argues that racial differences in IQ are entirely due to environmental factors.

What does this mean for traditional African Societies?

The conventional notion of African identity that was conceived in opposition to the West has proven to be self-limiting and helps to enforce unfavorable foreign stereotypes of who we as a people are.

Very often, African communities, shun their youth who attempt to integrate new cultures, insisting as if by force, that African young people must identify themselves with traditional African culture. This causes some form of intergenerational conflict which weakens our societal fabric. We should be able to reform African culture to suit a growing urban lifestyle.

When we identify ourselves solely by our culture, we rid ourselves of our true identity as one humanity with different forms of expression. Culture is not who we are, it's just a means we use to express ourselves.

The young generation is inspired by cultures that permit them to fully express themselves and grow, not by those that force them, to live up to standards of an expired century. African culture is valuable, but by remaining complacent or trying to keep our culture "Original", we have rid ourselves of the opportunity to evolve. Cultures must co-exist and inter-breathe.

Each culture must always have a core from which the pop-culture is derived, however its poor judgement to assume that everyone must belong to such core, and whoever doesn't belong shouldn't be welcome.

Culture is best preserved by being exploited. When we exploit our culture, it creates room for us to develop it further and to evolve as a people. Culture was made by man and should not become a prison for him.

6. QUOTES FROM ACROSS AFRICA

" I have taken particular interest in watching the performance of African teams at the Russia 2018 World Cup.

I have observed that even with so much attacking talent, African teams love to defend. It is as if they go into the game to maintain the same result before the game.

I have noted that their play is not different from the way most Africans approach life. Africans love to defend their status.

They keep unproductive pieces of land for generations, they shun business events, they defend irrelevant customs, traditions, they stick to economic activities that keep their poverty intact."

By Yasin Musa Ayami

"Culture is what has been encouraged to grow within me from an early age. When the baby body is gone and the adult body emerges then I must choose what I came to earth for;"

Etchi Juliette Besem Oben

"In the past, African music was in the world music category and I don't want to be pigeonholed in that world."

DJ and Entrepreneur Black Coffee

"some traditional practices cannot be demonstrated empirically and such go against the spirit of globalisation, science and technology. Therefore, negative and harmful traditional practices that dehumanise people and portray them as unimproved and backward people without future, should as a matter of urgency be discarded since culture is an adaptive system together with values that play a central role in giving the society its uniqueness"

Gabriel E. Idang

DIVINE VERKIJIKA

ABOUT THE AUTHOR

Divine Verkijika is a Cameroonian Artist and Sociocultural Activist
Author of: *The Failure of Oral Tradition: A case of African Beliefs &
Customs*